The ★ ♥
VLOGGERS
YEARBOOK

STUDIO

CONTENTS

HI GUYS!

HOW TO USE THIS BOOK

Look for these icons at the top of each page. They tell you what each vlogger likes to talk about.

 **Life** — All about life, advice, daily activities, friends and fun.

 **Fashion** — Fashion faves, lookbooks and high street hauls.

 **Comedy** — Pranks, fails and funnies. Vlogs to make you laugh!

 Gaming — Gaming let's plays, hacks and tips you NEED to know!

Beauty — Beauty tips and advice, how-to vlogs and beauty must-haves.

 **Music** — Singing, playing, writing and performing all kinds of music.

Science & Education — Experimenting, analysing and discovering awesome facts.

Travel — Seeing the world and discovering new places.

 CENSORED Warning! These vloggers swear ... a lot.

THE WONDERFUL WORLD OF VLOGGING

They feel like best friends, you can watch them whenever you want, wherever you want (with a little help from Wi-Fi or your mobile phone) and best of all they want to entertain you any way they can. They can make you laugh, cry or distract you from your day, but also inspire you to truly live your life. We salute the stars of YouTube and bring you this book so that you can discover more about the vloggers you love, the channels you should be following and how you can maybe even become the next big vlogging superstar yourself!

YOUTUBE IS AVAILABLE IN MORE THAN 61 LANGUAGES AND 75 COUNTRIES AROUND THE WORLD.

5 THINGS YOU SHOULD KNOW
before you turn the page ...

1. A vlog is a combination of a video and a blog.
2. A vlogger is the person who creates the vlog.
3. The website YouTube has the most video content (and vlogs) on the Internet.
4. You can search and watch videos and vlogs on YouTube for free and you don't need your own account to do so.
5. If you want to upload videos and vlogs yourself, you do need your own account, which is also free.

A HISTORY OF You

2005
YouTube is founded by Chad Hurley, Steve Chen and Jawed Karim, who were all early employees of PayPal.

2005
The first video is uploaded to YouTube. Called 'Me at the Zoo', it featured YT creator Jawed Karim at San Diego Zoo in the USA.

2006
YouTube becomes the fifth most popular website, with 100 million videos viewed daily and more than 65,000 new videos uploaded every day.

 6

The Professionals

Vloggers use anything and everything as inspiration for their video content: from news, shopping, films and games to their personal highs and lows. For some vloggers, making videos is just a fun hobby, but for the truly dedicated, like the superstars in this book, vlogging can turn into a very lucrative career. Many of the most subscribed-to vloggers are part of the YouTube Partner Program, which enables them to make money from their vlogs via adverts. Vloggers may start out online, but a few years and a few million subscribers later and these Internet superstars can soon become best-selling authors, TV personalities and, in some cases, even movie stars!

42% OF INTERNET USERS SAY THAT THEY'VE WATCHED A VLOG IN THE PAST MONTH.

3 GREAT THINGS about YouTube vlogs!

1. Anyone can make one!
2. It's a two-way street: a vlogger can chat to their audience, and, via social media, their audience can chat back.
3. Sometimes they can make lots of money!

TYPES OF VLOGGERS — 100%

- 10% brainiacs
- 20% gamers
- 20% pranksters
- 10% travel experts
- 10% shopaholics
- 20% beauty gurus
- 10% singers and actors

2007
be consumes as h bandwidth as tire Internet did he year 2000.

2012
Visitors to YouTube spend an average of 15 minutes a day on the site.

2013
Around 60 hours of new video are uploaded every minute, with a billion people viewing the site every month.

2014
YouTube has 300 hours of new videos uploaded to its site every minute.

2015
YouTube ranks as the third most visited website on the Internet, behind Google and Facebook.

7

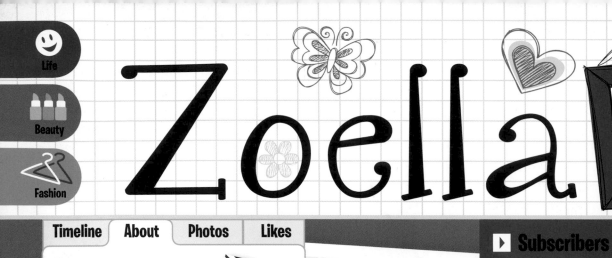

Zoella

QUEEN OF VLOGGING!

Timeline | **About** | **Photos** | **Likes**

Subscribers ▶ + 8.2 million

aka: Zoe Elizabeth Sugg

born: 28 March 1990

tagline: thoughts. fashion. beauty.

we ♥: her bubbly personality

she's like: the best big sis EVER

most likely to: say "Hellooo everyone!"

least likely to: give bad advice

" JUST SAY YES! "

" Focus on what matters. "

2009
Creates her blog 'Zoella' and uploads her first YouTube vlog. Has 1000 followers by the end of the year.

2011
Wins Cosmopolitan's 'Best Established Beauty Blog' award, and wins 'Best Beauty Vlogger' award the following year.

2013
Voted 'Best British Vlogger' at the Radio 1 Teen Awards in both 2013 and 2014.

2013
Reaches 1 million subscribers.

2014
Wins Teen Choice Award for 'Choice Web Star: Fashion/Beauty'.

BIO

Zoe Sugg is an Internet megastar who started her YouTube channel 'Zoella' back in 2009 to share her love of all things beauty and fashion with the online world. With her cheery personality, friendly tips and willingness to look wacky in front of the camera, it's not hard to see why this girl is the current queen of cyberspace! Zoella's channel has over 450 million video views (A LOT!) and her first book, 'Girl Online', sold more copies in its first week than any other debut author in history!

SHHHH!

Rumour has it there is a bidding war to turn Zoella's book, 'Girl Online', into a film. Who's going to play Penny?

Nala

PET PALS

Zoe has two guinea pigs called Pippin and Percy, and an adorable pug called Nala!

▶ TOP WATCH...

How To: My Quick and Easy Hairstyles + 9.7 million views

Zoe is a girl of many talents! In 2014 she launched her own beauty brand, Zoella Beauty.

Zoella gave up her day job at New Look in 2012 to focus on her vlogging

10% fussy eater

15% Disney DVD collector

30% high-street hero

100% GIRL ONLINE!

5% pizza & cupcake addict

10% animal mad

10% Zalfie

20% best friend

FOLLOW HER ...

 Zoella, MoreZoella

 @ZozeeBo

 @zozeebo

 /zoe.zoella

"DO THINGS FOR YOU AND NOT FOR ANYBODY ELSE."

2014
Named as the first 'Digital Ambassador' for Mind, the mental health charity.

2014
Reaches 5 million subscribers, and releases her debut novel, 'Girl Online', on 25th November.

2015
Named 'Most Inspirational Woman of the Decade' in Technology by Grazia magazine.

2015
Waxwork figures of her and boyfriend Alfie Deyes are created by Madame Tussaud's in London.

2015
All set for the release in October or November of a sequel novel to 'Girl Online'.

Pointless Blog Alfie

KING OF VLOGS!

Timeline | **About** | **Photos** | **Likes**

aka: Alfred Sydney Deyes

born: 17 September 1993

tagline: Do more of what makes you happy.

we ♥ : his silly stunts

he's like: perfect boyfriend material

most likely to: have a laugh

least likely to: leave his phone at home

Subscribers + 4.1 million

ALCATEL onetouch

"WHAT'S UP, GUYS!"

Alfie's first book, 'The Pointless Book' raced straight to the top of the best-sellers list... ...and so did his second book, 'The Pointless Book 2'!

" Nothing is impossible, even the word spells I'm possible!"

 2009
Begins his PointlessBlog YouTube channel.

 2013
Announces on 25th August that he and Zoe are officially a couple.

2013
Becomes a member of the 'Guinness World Records OMG!' channel and holds a number of world records.

 2014
His first book, 'The Pointless Book', publishes in September.

Alfie loves to collab' with his YouTuber mates, including ThatcherJoe, Jim Chapman, Caspar Lee, SprinkleofGlitter, Tanya Burr, Troye Sivan and Marcus Butler. He's even made videos with Ariana Grande!

SHHHH!

Alfie has hinted at a new project in the pipeline that will be a real game changer. What could it be?

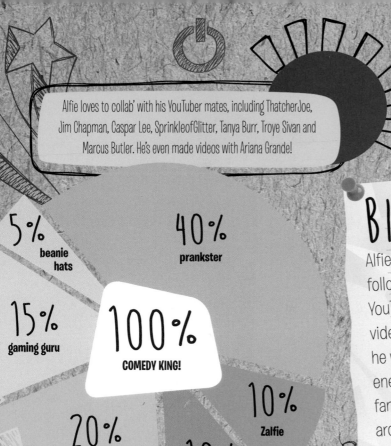

5%
beanie hats

40%
prankster

15%
gaming guru

100%
COMEDY KING!

20%
challenges

10%
animal mad

10%
Zalfie

BIO

Alfie Deyes has gained a huge YouTube following thanks to his PointlessBlog, a YouTube channel he has uploaded daily video diaries to (well, nearly every day) since he was 15! This chirpy Brighton boy is high in energy and loves to chat, offer advice to his fans, post funny vlogs of himself messing around in the Brighton 'Zalfie Pad' with girlfriend Zoella, do silly challenges with his mates or pull 'pointless' stunts like shaving his armpits!

ZALFIE

CUTE COUPLE ALERT!

FOLLOW HIM ...

▶ PointlessBlog, PointlessBlogVlogs, PointlessBlogGames

🐦 @PointlessBlog

📷 @pointlessblog

f /PointlessBlogTV

Most likely to...
get married to his super-famous girlfriend Zoella and live happily ever after in Brighton with their puglicious puppy, Nala.

Alfie likes to call his fans
'chumps'!

2014
Sings on Band Aid's 'Do They Know it's Christmas?' single.

2015
Moves into a house in Brighton, UK with his girlfriend Zoella, dubbed as the 'Zalfie Pad'.

2015
Releases 'The Pointless Book 2' on 26th March, with 'The Pointless Book 3' set for release in late 2015.

2015
Gets his own waxwork at Madame Tussaud's London, along with girlfriend Zoella.

LIVE ON STAGE

Check out these dates for your vlogging diary.

AMITY FEST

It's all in the name! Amity means 'good relationship' and this is what the British YouTube stars want with their fans. Touring locations around the UK, Britain's top vloggers step out from behind their webcams and onto the stage, giving UK fans a taste of festival fun.

When: Watch this space.
Best for: Those who think Brits are best!

SUMMER IN THE CITY

The UK's largest YouTube convention is an annual event in London open to anyone, whether they are YouTube creators, viewers or professionals. With live chats, meet-and-greets and stalls, it's a must-visit event for vlogging devotees.

When: August.
Best for: UK-based fans.

YOUTUBE FANFEST

YouTube's own convention. #YTFF brings YouTube's stars from around the world together for unique live shows on stage. Enjoy the thrilling and creative mix of music, comedy, dance and fashion – an unmissable show you'll never forget.

When: All year.
Best for: Any YouTube fan.

BUFFER FESTIVAL

Buffer Festival is YouTube's answer to the Cannes Film Festival. The event plays host to a variety of vloggers, writers, directors and creative types from all around the world, showcasing their work over three days in Toronto, Canada.

When: Autumn.
Best for: Creative types.

DIGITOUR

DigiTour Media is a touring music and social media festival with events held in the USA and Canada in all kinds of venues, from theatres to fields. The tour began as a showcase for stars from YouTube, but its performers now include Vine, Twitter, Instagram and music stars too.

When: Summer.
Best for: Social media and music fans.

VIDCON

Ok, so you'll need to fly to LA, California, but true fans will want to make the trip to this annual convention that allows content creators and viewers to share ideas. The first VidCon was held back in 2010 and is now the biggest gathering of Internet creators and viewers in the world.

When: Usually July.
Best for: Getting selfies with the stars.

DON'T MISS!

Check out and vote for your favourite vloggers in these top awards ceremonies held throughout the year.

Shorty Awards   **Streamys**

BBC Radio 1's Teen Awards

The Webby Awards

Nickelodeon Kids' Choice Awards

nigahiga

CENSORED

THE CHARACTER

Timeline | **About** | Photos | Likes

aka: Ryan Higa

born: 6 June 1990

tagline: Posted a video on YouTube over 7 years ago thinking no one would see it.

we 🖤 : his crazy impressions

he's like: funny but clever at the same time

most likely to: make fun of celebs

least likely to: keep his feelings to himself

▶ **Subscribers**   **+ 14.6 million**

Ryan has a black belt in Judo!

Ryan studied Nuclear Medicine at university before dropping out to be a full-time vlogger.

"I am who I am because of you."

20% happy

30% multiple personalities including **Regina, R-Dizzle** and **Hanate**

5% confessions

100% COOL!

10% whizz-kid

35% ranting

BIO

This hilarious vlogging star first launched his channel in 2006, uploading lip-syncing videos before moving quickly on to spoofs, rants, music videos and comedy vlogs, which are now viewed and laughed at all over the world. He has more than 2.5 BILLION video views on his main channel, is the 10th most subscribed-to creator on YouTube, and has even created a feature-length film!

FOLLOW HIM ...

▶ nigahiga, HigaTV

🐦 @TheRealRyanHiga

📷 @notryanhiga

f /higatv

In 2010, nigahiga was the first YouTube channel to reach 3 million subscribers.

SMOSH

THE BEST BUDS!

Timeline | About | Photos | Likes

aka: Ian Andrew Hecox and Anthony Padilla

born: 30 November 1987 and 16 September 1987

tagline: Bringing you Smoshy Goodness!

we ♥ **:** their silly toilet humour

they're like: your totally bonkers buddies

most likely to: make a spoof vlog

least likely to: run out of funny ideas

▶ **Subscribers** + 20 million

"DANGER IS MY MIDDLE NAME."

"SHUT UP!"

"I LEARNED HOW TO SURVIVE UNDERWATER: by holding my breath!"

2002
www.smosh.com is launched.

2005
The pair start posting videos on YouTube, and Smosh quickly becomes one of the most popular channels.

2009
Their website smosh.com has a big makeover with a new games section and extra videos.

2010
The iShut Up app is launched.

BIO

The epic combination of scripted scenes, crazy costumes, funny songs, improvisations, movie spoofs and wacky challenges have rocketed this comedy team to YouTube fame and fortune. Fans love their unique brand of unpredictable but harmless humour, not to mention their cute haircuts. They are now set to entertain millions more with the release of 'Smosh: The Movie'.

Smosh has been the #1 most subscribed channel on YouTube on 3 separate occasions.

10% generous

20% lip-syncing

15% crazy

100% BEST BUDS!

25% food battles

30% besties

"LET'S DO SOME MANLY STUFF!"

The original Smosh channel was formed in 2005, with the boys lip-syncing to cartoon theme songs like Pokémon and Power Rangers (which you can still find online).

They've come a long way since then, with multiple Smosh-related channels including gaming, animation, and French and Spanish-dubbed videos.

Ian and Anthony met at school when they were just 11 years old.

SMOSH HAVE RELEASED 4 ALBUMS OF THEIR ORIGINAL SONGS TO DATE.

FOLLOW THEM ...

▶ Smosh, Smosh 2nd Channel, Smosh Games, Shut Up! Cartoons, Smosh France

🐦 @smosh

📷 @smosh

f /smosh

2012
The boys start three new YouTube channels- ElSmosh, Shut Up! Cartoons and Smosh Games.

2013
The Smosh French channel is launched, showing Smosh videos with French subtitles.

2014
Smosh Games wins the Streamy Award for 'Best Gaming Channel, Show or Series'.

2015
The pair release their teen comedy film, 'Smosh: The Movie' in July, as well as a series of comics at the end of the year.

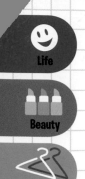
Life

Beauty

Fashion

Tanya Burr

THE BEAUTY PRINCESS!

"Be **BRIGHT**! Be **HAPPY**! Be **YOU**!"

Timeline | **About** | **Photos** | **Likes**

aka: Tanya Burr

born: 9 June 1989

tagline: I upload a mixture of fashion, make-up, baking and other random videos.

we 🖤 : her amazing make-up tips

she's like: the friendliest vlogger ever

most likely to: get her beauty hauls from the High Street

least likely to: have a bad word to say about anyone

Tanya is a trained make-up artist.

▶ **Subscribers** | + 2.7 million

"PEOPLE SAY THAT WHEN THEY WATCH MY VIDEOS THEY FEEL LIKE THEY'RE MY FRIEND 🖤 AND I LOVE THAT."

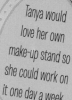
Tanya would love her own make-up stand so she could work on it one day a week.

" Be a WARRIOR, not a worrier!"

2009
Joins YouTube in October.

2012
Sits on the judging panel for glossy mag ELLE's Beauty Awards.

2012
Gets engaged to fellow vlogger Jim Chapman.

BIO

Tanya Burr's tutorials covering celeb make-up, beauty hauls, hairstyles and product reviews make her a must-follow vlogger for anyone looking for some serious style and beauty inspo. We love her easy-to-follow tips, positive attitude and friendly personality, and we're not the only ones – she counts fellow vlogging star Zoe Sugg as one of her besties! Tanya's online popularity has exploded into the offline world as well, with the launch of her own nail varnish and lip gloss lines, regular columns for popular mags like Grazia and even her own book, 'Love, Tanya'.

10% fashion lover

15% obsessed with nail polish

5% afraid of the dark

10% Harry Potter addict

100% GORGEOUS!

5% great friend

10% brilliant baker

45% beauty guru

FOLLOW HER ...

▶ Tanya Burr

🐦 @TanyaBurr

📷 @tanyaburr

f /OfficialTanyaBurr

TANYA STARTED VLOGGING AFTER JIM'S MAKE-UP ARTIST SISTERS (AND FELLOW YOUTUBERS) @PIXIWOO TAUGHT HER ABOUT MAKE-UP AND PERSUADED HER TO MAKE HER OWN CHANNEL!

GUESS WHOSE BOYFRIEND IS ON PAGE 18!

▶ TOP WATCH...

Tanya Burr & Zoella 3 Minute Makeup Challenge!
+ 2.8 million views

SHHHH!
Tanya has confessed she would love to be on 'Strictly Come Dancing'. **Watch this space!**

2013

Enlisted as a judge for the Grazia Beauty Awards .

2014
Launches Tanya Burr Cosmetics online and at Superdrug, and creates her own fashion edit for very.co.uk.

2015

Releases her first book, 'Love, Tanya' in January.

JIM CHAPMAN

THE GENTLEMAN!

| Timeline | **About** | Photos | Likes |

aka: James Alfred Chapman

born: 28 December 1987

tagline: Internet friend!

we ❤ **:** his amazing sense of style

he's like: totally swoonsome

most likely to: vlog every day

least likely to: ever be grumpy

▶ **Subscribers** + 2.3 million

"HELLO BEST FRIENDS!"

"I look **pretty ALL** the time!"

"DON'T GIVE IN to peer pressure!"

BIO

Jim Chapman considers his job the best in the world, that's because he's had some awful ones! After graduating in 2009, Jim struggled to find his calling, working in insurance before YouTube stardom beckoned. Encouraged by Tanya and inspired by her success, Jim decided to get online and start vlogging. Starting with fashion and men's grooming, Jim now vlogs about anything he feels like, from cake-making fails to tips on making friends and we love him for it.

CUTE COUPLE ALERT!

FAMILY VLOGGERS!

Jim's sisters Sam and Nic Chapman are the popular beauty vloggers PixiWoo. He also has a twin brother called John, who co-runs the Lean Machines YouTube channel!

Ridiculously cute couple **Jim** and **Tanya** (Janya) got engaged in 2012, after Jim whisked Tanya off to her fave city, New York, and proposed **(watch the 'WE'RE ENGAGED' vid on Jim's channel)**. The two lovebirds were at the same school but it wasn't until 2007 when they met at a party in their local village that Tanya first noticed Jim's gentlemanly ways. Their first date was at the cinema but Jim was too shy to give Tanya a **kiss** goodnight, so she dived in for a quick peck before hopping on the bus home. **Go Tan!**

FOLLOW HIM ...

▶ **Jim Chapman, EverydayJim**

🐦 **@JimsTweetings**

📷 **@jimalfredchapman**

f **/OfficialJimChapman**

THATCHER Joe

WARNING: HYPER ALERT!

Life

Gaming

Comedy

BEST IMPRESSIONS!

| Timeline | **About** | Photos | Likes |

aka: Joseph Graham Sugg

born: 8 September 1991

tagline: Likes to make a fool out of himself on camera for your entertainment.

we 🖤 : awesome celeb impressions

he's like: the brother we always wanted

most likely to: be goofy on camera

least likely to: take himself seriously

▶ **Subscribers** **+ 4.6 million**

Pie chart:
- 10% best roomie ever
- 10% best bro ever
- 10% good singer
- 20% hyperactive
- 5% penguin fan
- 100% FUN!
- 15% collaborator
- 30% prankster

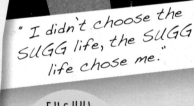

" I didn't choose the SUGG life, the SUGG life chose me."

BIO

It's no big surprise that Joe Sugg (aka ThatcherJoe, aka Zoella's brother) has managed to follow in his big sister's footsteps to become a much-loved and laughed-at vlogging star. His entertaining channel is packed with inventive challenges, pranks and 'unique' impressions (Kim Kardashian, anyone?). This boy will literally go to any lengths to make a fool out of himself for your laughs!

TOP WATCH...

More Amazing Impressions + 5.7 million views

EUGHH!
Joe claims to like eating lemons with the peel on!

FOLLOW HIM ...

▶ ThatcherJoe, ThatcherJoeVlogs, ThatcherJoeGames

🐦 @Joe_Sugg

📷 @joe_sugg

f /ThatcherJoe

SHHHH!
Joe still runs up the stairs in the dark!

BEFORE YOUTUBE ... Joe did a thatching apprenticeship, which inspired his YouTube name, ThatcherJoe.

2011
In November, Joe creates his ThatcherJoe channel on YouTube.

2013
In January, Joe adds a second channel, ThatcherJoe Vlogs to his YouTube portfolio.

2013
Creates a gaming channel in May called ThatcherJoe Games.

2013
Reaches 1 million subscribers on his main channel in November.

2014
Moves to London with fellow YouTuber Caspar Lee.

2015
Lands a role voicing a seagull called Kyle in 'The SpongeBob Movie: Sponge Out of Water'.

2015
Watch out for the release of his first book in September – a graphic novel!

A-Z OF VLOGGING!

A IS FOR AMERICA
Loads of our fave vloggers are based in the USA: Tyler Oakley; Joey Graceffa; Jenna Marbles; Miranda Sings ... need we go on?

B IS FOR BROTHERS
Vloggers Joe Sugg and Jim Chapman both followed in their older siblings' vlogging footsteps.

C IS FOR COLLABORATIONS
Vloggers love to collab' with other YouTube creators. It's one big vlogging community!

D IS FOR DRAW MY LIFE
The draw my life tag is an essential YouTube upload, where vloggers narrate their life stories with stick people drawings! Short, visual and honest, it's the perfect way to get to know your fave YouTubers.

E IS FOR EDITING
Truly talented vloggers can chat to camera for hours on end, but also need a bit of handy editing to keep the very best bits just for you.

F IS FOR FANDOMS
Fans can't get enough of their fave vloggers and show up in their hordes to meet-and-greets. The Bro Army, Sugglets, Chumps - which fandom do you belong to?

G IS FOR GAMING
From PewDiePie to Stampylonghead, gaming fans flock to YouTube, not only to find out about the latest games, but also to watch their heroes play them.

H IS FOR HAULS
Always a crowd pleaser and a must-do vlog for all fashion and beauty YouTubers.

I IS FOR INTERNET
What would we do without it?

J IS FOR JOKES
Whether it's with pranks, sketches, funny songs or just being all-round hilarious human beings, the top comedy vloggers will make you laugh till you cry.

K IS FOR KEEP AT IT
Caspar Lee's top tip for aspiring YouTubers is to "keep persevering". Success doesn't just happen overnight on YouTube, you know.

L IS FOR LONDON
Home to many of the British YouTube crew and location of YT convention, Summer in the City.

M IS FOR **MOST SUBSCRIBED**

PewDiePie is the undisputed King of YouTube with the most subscribers in the world and his Bro Army is still growing!

N IS FOR **NEW CONTENT**

Vloggers need to be creative and come up with fun new ideas for their vlogs to keep their viewers entertained.

O IS FOR **ONLINE**

Whether they're uploading new vlogs, posting pics, tweeting news or engaging with their fans, vloggers are online most of the time.

P IS FOR **PETS**

From guinea pigs to pugs, kittens to lizards - loads of your favourite vloggers are purrfectly potty about pets.

Q IS FOR **QUILT**

Essential vlog viewing equipment. Who doesn't love to curl up under a cosy quilt and catch up on the all the latest uploads?

R IS FOR **RANDOM**

And it is, all of it! From bonkers pranks to shop-tastic hauls, vlogger's content is totally random most of the time, and you love them for it!

S IS FOR **SUBSCRIBERS**

It's a numbers game. The more you have, the bigger you'll be.

T IS FOR **TWITTER**

Vloggers love to keep in touch with their fans on Twitter, so check out their tweets too to keep up with all the latest news.

U IS FOR **UPLOADING**

YouTube has more than 1 billion users, all uploading, viewing and sharing content. That's an awful lot of vlogging going on!

V IS FOR **VLOGGING!**

Video + blogging = vlogging! It's the television of the interweb, and there's nothing we'd rather watch!

W IS FOR **WRITING**

They're on your mobiles, laptops, tablets and now they're on your bookshelves too. Nothing beats a good read... except perhaps a good read penned by your favourite YouTube star!

X IS FOR **X-RATED**

Some vloggers occasionally use naughty language in their videos. Yes, it's true - we're looking at you, Pewds!

Y IS FOR **YOUTUBE** (OBVS!)

The number one place to be if you're a vlogger, and every vlogger's favourite website.

Z IS FOR **'ZALFIE'**

Vlogging power couple (and cutest couple) of the moment.

PEWDIEPIE

CENSORED

Timeline | **About** | Photos | Likes

aka: Felix Arvid Ulf Kjellberg

born: 24 October 1989

tagline: I love all my bros!

we ♥: he always speaks his mind

he's like: the most fun ever

most likely to: make you want to play computer games

least likely to: turn off his computer ever

▶ Subscribers | + 37 million

KING OF GAMING

MOST POPULAR VLOGGER!

"I DON'T CAAAAARE!"

PewDiePie picks up one subscriber per minute!

" Stay awesome bros, I know you will."

#BROARMY

2009
Joins YouTube.

2011
Leaves university, where he was studying Economics and Technology, to focus on his YouTube career after attracting hundreds of thousands of subscribers.

2011
Fellow vlogger Marzia Bisognin sends PewDiePie a fan message in June. After months of chatting online, PewDiePie meets Marzia in Italy in October, and she soon becomes his girlfriend.

BIO

He may be just a guy from Sweden who likes making vlogs, but his crazy approach to reviewing video and mobile games has made PewDiePie the number one vlogger on YouTube, with over 35 million subscribers! His hilarious facial and vocal reactions to the games that he plays have not only made him a worldwide star, but also influenced the games industry, with developers making games that are not just fun to play, but fun to watch being played too!

His first channel was called PewDie but he forgot the password so created a new one with pie at the end, cos he loves pie!

20% fun

15% generous

10% arty

5% guitar player

100% WEB RULER!

10% animal mad

40% gaming guru

"HOW TO RECORD YOUTUBE GAME PLAY VIDEO TUTORIAL BY ME."

FOLLOW HIM …

▶ PewDiePie

🐦 @pewdiepie

📷 @felixkjellberg

f /PewDiePie

TOP WATCH…

A Funny Montage
+ 64 million hits

The one where he screams A LOT!

Before we begin we must make sure we have the proper equipment:
- 1 Elgato gameplay capture card
- a wire thing
- 2 x USB power cables
- some cat fertiliser
- a hammer

(If you don't have any of these, don't worry, they are completely useless.)

1. Read the serial number on the back of your box.

2. Take your hammer and bash the box up.

3. Now you can proceed to making CoD videos.

CUTE COUPLE ALERT!

Fashion YouTuber Marzia **@CutiePieMarzia,** was a PewDiePie fan before becoming his girlfriend. The popular pair now live together in England and have two pugs.

Most likely to…
collaborate on gaming vlogs together.

2013
In December, becomes the most subscribed to YouTube channel in the world.

2014
Voted 'Most Popular Gaming Web Star' at the Teen Choice Awards.

WATCH THIS SPACE!

23

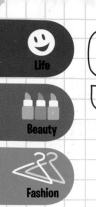

SPRINKLE of Glitter

THE GIRLIEST GIRL!

Timeline **About** **Photos** **Likes**

Louise is a graduate of Liverpool John Moores University.

▶ **Subscribers** + 2.2 million

aka: Louise Alexandra Watson (was Pentland)

born: 28 April 1985

tagline: I love beauty, babies (particularly mine) and shopping.

we ♥: her warm personality

she's like: a ray of sunshine

most likely to: chatter the night away

least likely to: have a moan

Louise has a little girl called Darcy, who often features in her videos.

30% beauty & shopping

10% sparkly gems

5% pink

100% GIRLY!

20% happy mummy vlogger

15% interior design

20% chummy advice

BIO
Following her successful Sprinkleofglitter blog, Louise launched her YouTube channel in 2010 and posts shopping, beauty, motivational and advice vlogs for her large sprinkling of fans. Following in the footsteps of her bestie Zoella, Louise is releasing her debut book 'Life with a Sprinkle of Glitter' in July 2015.

"WOAH PONY! That's exciting."

FOLLOW HER ...

▶ Sprinkleofglitter, SprinkleofChatter

🐦 @SprinkleofGlitr

📷 @sprinkleofglitr

f /sprinkleofglitter

" *ALOHA Sprinklerinos!*"

BESTEST CHUMS
Louise's bestie is fellow beauty vlogger, Zoella!
* Their friendship began with an email from Louise to Zoella telling her she loved her vlog back in 2009.
* In 2010, Louise sent Zoella a sweet little present to thank her for all her entertaining vlogs.
* They messaged each other every day for months, before finally meeting at an Eyeko (make-up) Event.
* The two friends love to collab in Chummy Chatter vlogs on Louise's second channel, talking about all things beauty, body image and boys.

Life

Beauty

Michelle Phan

MOST POPULAR BEAUTY VLOGGER!

"**I live**, **I love**, **I teach**, but mostly **I learn**."

| Timeline | **About** | Photos | Likes |

▶ **Subscribers** + 7.8 million

aka: Michelle Phan

born: 11 April 1987

tagline: Sit back, enjoy and let's play with make-up!

we ♥ **:** her amazing make-up tips

she's like: SUPER glam

most likely to: teach you how to look glam

least likely to: give up on her dreams

"I'M PASSIONATE ABOUT TEACHING OTHERS HOW TO LOOK AND FEEL FABULOUS IN THEIR OWN SKIN."

FOLLOW HER ...

▶ **Michelle Phan**

🐦 **@MichellePhan**

📷 **@michellephan**

f **/MichellePhanOfficial**

BIO

Michelle Phan is a digital pioneer and one of the earliest beauty vloggers on YouTube. She's since uploaded over 300 vlogs, has more than 1 billion video views, and has made her name as one of the top beauty influencers online, teaching more people how to "become their own best make-up artist" than anyone else in the world! Her signature vids are cool, arty and expertly edited, with clear, easy-to-follow instructions. Check out her popular Halloween themed videos for some super spooky beauty tips.

10% determined
15% teacher
100% GLAM!
25% entrepreneur
15% dreamer
10% artistic
25% make-up inspo

NOT JUST A PRETTY FACE...

Trailblazing the way for girl vloggers everywhere, Michelle is the founder of FAWN (For All Women Network) and also co-founder of ipsy.com, an online site for beauty lovers. She's even launched her own make-up line with L'Oreal!

DID YOU KNOW?
Michelle originally wanted to work as an artist for Disney Pixar or Dreamworks.

2005
Creates a personal blog posting different make-up tutorials.

2007
Posts her first make-up tutorial on YouTube in May.

2009/10
Buzzfeed features two of her Lady Gaga make-up tutorials, which helps them go viral.

2010
Lancôme make Michelle their official video make-up artist after she features their products in her videos.

2013
L'Oreal launches Michelle's cosmetic line in August, called 'Em Cosmetics'.

2014
Is awarded with first ever Streamy 'ICON Award' for Inspiration.

2014
Releases her book in October, 'Make Up: Your Life Guide to Beauty, Style and Success - Online and Off.'

2014
Launches her own music label with Cutting Edge Music.

25

Life

Comedy

Music

Shane Dawson

CENSORED

Timeline   **About**   **Photos**   **Likes**

Subscribers + 6.6 million

aka: Shane Lee Yaw

born: 19 July 1988

tagline: I hate myselfie.

we ♥: his honesty

he's like: the loudest vlogger ever

most likely to: offend a celeb

least likely to: worry about offending anyone

His gf is fellow YouTuber **Lisbug**, who has over 1 million followers herself!

25%
multiple personalities
(Shanaynay, Ned the Nerd, S-Deezy, Mom, Aunt Hilda, Fruit Lupe and Amy)

10%
honest

10%
actor

10%
writer

100%
OUTRAGEOUS!

15%
outrageous

20%
funny

10%
a bit shouty

" Be you. "

He's scarily good at acting too, and appeared in the horror film, **Smiley.**

BIO

What started off as Shane's hobby is now his full-time job. Fans can't get enough of his outrageous vlogs on his three YouTube channels – packed with music video spoofs, impersonations, colourful characters and crazy commentaries on everything celebrity and Internet related. Oozing with confidence, it's hard to believe this Californian heart-throb was once bullied at school, but he's definitely having the last laugh now and will no doubt keep on laughing with his legions of loyal fans.

PET PALS

Animal-lover Shane has lots of pets – four dogs, named Miley, Charlie, Chocolate and Unicorn (aka Corny), and two cats, named Muffins and Snoop.

FOLLOW HIM ...

▶ **ShaneDawsonTV, shane**

🐦 **@shanedawson**

📷 **@shanedawson**

f **/shanedawsonfans**

2008
In March, creates his first YouTube channel: ShaneDawson TV.

2010
Wins a Teen Choice Award in the category 'Choice Web Star'.

2010
Wins a Streamy Award for 'Best Vlogger'.

2012
Begins a music career and has since released six singles.

2014
Stars in his own movie 'Not Cool' and writes his first book, 'I Hate Myselfie: A Collection of Essays'.

26

CENSORED

Jenna Marbles

COMEDY QUEEN!

Timeline | **About** | Photos | Likes

aka: Jenna N. Mourey

born: 15 September 1986

tagline: I like to make magical videos on the Internet machine.

we ♥ : that she's SO real

she's like: your straight-talking bestie

most likely to: throw them THE FACE

least likely to: be serious even for a second

▶ **Subscribers** + 15 million

" I'm silly and fun. Because that's how I choose to view the world."

25% hilarious

20% dog lover

100% FUNNY!

% impersonations

10% unicorn

15% tells it how it is

25% silly

PET PALS

Jenna has two awesome dogs named Mr Marbles (her YouTube name is a mix of her name and Marbles') and Kermit, who appear in most of her videos. She adopted a new dog called Peach in 2014 with her boyfriend, Julien.

"DON'T EVER, EVER, EVER GIVE UP. YOU'RE HERE FOR A REASON, EVEN IF IT'S JUST TO LOOK AT CATS ON THE INTERNET."

BIO

Undoubtedly the comedy queen of the vloggers, Jenna Marbles is adored and followed by teens across the globe. Almost an overnight success, her video 'How to Trick People into Thinking You're Good-Looking' went viral with more than 5 million hits in its first week (it now has over 60 million views!). From there she's soared to superstar heights and become the most followed female in the world. This girl is sassy, inventive, super funny and more than a little bit rude.

She's clever too! Jenna has a degree in Psychology and a Masters in Sports Psychology.

TOP WATCH...

How to Talk To Animals

+ 7 million views

FOLLOW HER ...

 JennaMarbles

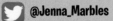 @Jenna_Marbles

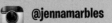 @jennamarbles

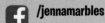 /jennamarbles

27

Life

Comedy

If you've never heard of **Dan and Phil**, these are two SuperTubers you need to subscribe to immediately.
They film quirky comedy videos, wacky challenges and tackle important topics such as how to appropriately eat a Pop-Tart, earning them a following of over 8 million subscribers collectively.

danisnot onfire

THE SLIGHTLY AWKWARD ONE!

Timeline	**About**	Photos	Likes

▶ **Subscribers** + 4.8 million

aka: Daniel James Howell

born: 11 June 1991

tagline: I make videos about how awkward I am and people laugh at me.

we ♥ : his quirky awkwardness

he's like: bursting with funniness

most likely to: do a dance in front of the camera

least likely to: try to be like anyone else

Dan's fans are called **Danosaurs** or **Dantarays**, who as a group are part of the **'Llamarmy'**.

Dan is 6ft 3in tall.

DAN = INTERNET CULT LEADER

"Do whatever you have to do to be happy."

BIO

Dan took a while to find his true calling in life, working in a number of jobs in supermarkets and DIY stores before a brief stint at Manchester University studying law. In 2009, on the advice of his best bud Phil, he posted his first video 'HELLO INTERNET' on YouTube. Now he is known around the world for his awesome channel, danisnotonfire, his good looks and his likeable personality.

Dan was once voted '**Hottest Lad of the Year**' by readers of web magazine Sugarscape.

DANTEASERS

Dan really, really likes Maltesers.

40% funny

10% Muse fan

100% LEADER!

10% Phan (Dan and Phil)

10% llama lover

10% gamer

20% Delia Smith addict

 2006
Dan and Phil join YouTube. (Dan doesn't post his first solo video until 2009.)

 2013
Get their own BBC Radio 1 show in January, called Dan and Phil.

2013
The boys interview Fall Out Boy on tour in April.

 2013
Win a Sony Golden Headphones Award for 'UK's favourite Radio Presenters'.

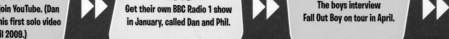
*"You aren't a professional Internet user until you understand how **haha** and **lol** have different meanings and appropriate uses."*

AmazingPhil

"RAWR!"

Timeline | **About** | **Photos** | **Likes**

aka: Philip Michael Lester

born: 30 January 1987

tagline: That guy with the hair from YouTube and Radio 1.

we ♥ : his innocent nature

he's like: a really fast talker

most likely to: teach you how to draw perfect cat whiskers

least likely to: always understand what you're on about

Phil is 6ft 2in tall.

He calls his fans **Phillions**.

BIO

Phil posted his first video when he was 19 and has been vlogging on his channel, AmazingPhil ever since. He has also found time to squeeze in a degree in English Language and Linguistics, and a Masters in Video Production. His channel has allowed him to turn his considerable talents to radio shows, movie appearances and adverts too. Phil truly **is** amazing!

FOLLOW THEM ...

▶ Danisnotonfire, AmazingPhil, DanAndPhilGAMES

🐦 @AmazingPhil, @danisnotonfire

📷 @amazingphil, @danisnotonfire

f /AmazingPhil, /danisnotonfire

His favourite animals are **lions** (he has a little lion teddy called Lion in the background of his videos).

▶ **Subscribers** + 2.5 million

" It's a good thing to be strange. Normalness leads to sadness."

▶ TOP WATCH...

Two boys ... one Sharpie ... 6 years of whiskers.

Phil is not on fire 6 + 4.5 million views

2014
In May, the pair launch DanandPhilGAMES - a new YouTube channel where they rate and review video games.

2014
The pair play cameo roles in the UK version of Disney's 'Big Hero 6' as Technicians 1 and 2.

2015
Create YouTube content for The BRIT Awards 2015.

2015
Release their book, 'The Amazing Book is not on Fire'.

29

Life

Comedy

Tyler Oakley

CENSORED

INTERNET HERO!

Timeline | **About** | **Photos** | **Likes**

aka: Tyler Oakley

born: 22 March 1989

tagline: Shameless self-promoter.

we ❤ : him just for being him

he's like: a cool and caring friend

most likely to: stand up for what he believes in

least likely to: keep quiet on the big issues

▶ **Subscribers** + 7 million

ONE OF THE LOUDEST VOICES ON YOUTUBE

" Care less about what other people think."

2007
Starts his first YouTube channel while still a student at Michegan State University.

2013
Reaches 1 million subscribers in June.

2013
Starts co-hosting Top That, a pop-culture news update for PopSugar.

PROFESSIONAL
Fangirl!

Tyler is a mega fan of Darren Criss, Lady Gaga, Betty Who and, of course, **One Direction**.

BROMANCE!
One of Tyler's best buds is Troye Sivan, and their hilarious videos as 'Troyler' have won them an army of fans. Face painting anyone?

5% social media

20% **LOUD** and proud

10% caring

10% Disney lover

100% **HERO!**

10% collaborator

5% Taco Bell addict

15% pizza fan

15% fun

10% loves his mum

BIO

With his trademark colourful hair and black-framed glasses, this inspirational vlogger likes to use his popularity and influence for good and is a hero to his millions of fans. Tech-savvy and super-witty Tyler vlogs about some hard-hitting topics, but he's also known for his love of pop culture and his hilarious videos and collaborations. His rise to fame can be credited to his likeable, kind and caring nature, but also his tough streak – he never backs down and always fights for what he believes in.

Tyler's a leading **LGBT** activist and speaks out on behalf of gay youth.

He has met the US President Barack Obama, and interviewed the First Lady about education issues.
GO TYLER!

DID YOU KNOW?
Tyler first started his YouTube channel as a way of keeping in touch with his three best friends from school.

FOLLOW HIM ...

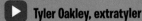 **Tyler Oakley, extratyler**

 @tyleroakley

 @tyleroakley

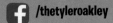 **/thetyleroakley**

2014
Wins 'Best Male Blogger' at the YouTube Entertainment Awards and 'Webstar: Male' at the Teen Choice Awards.

2015
Interviews celebs on the red carpet at the 2015 Grammy Awards.

LET'S GO LOUD!

31

HOW TO BE A VLOGGING SUPERSTAR

Whether you want to become a YouTube star, or you just have something you'd like to share with the world, check out these top tips on vlogging from the people who know (and do it) best!

What you'll need:

1. A camera for filming (your mobile phone should do).
2. A computer to edit your videos on.
3. Editing software (free ones like Movie Maker or iMovie are a good place to start).
4. An Internet connection.
5. A YouTube channel to upload your vlogs and videos to.
6. Something to say.
7. Time and dedication.
8. Fairy lights (just kidding, you don't really need these, but lots of vloggers love them!)

How to do it:

Make sure your camera is filming in landscape mode (turn your phone on its side), and ensure your camera is set to film in widescreen if possible. This means that there are no black bars around your video when you edit and upload it to YouTube.

Make sure you think about the sound as well as the picture. It's all well and good filming an amazing chat to the camera when you are outside, but if it's windy or noisy no one will be able to hear you.

Sometimes it's good to write an outline of what you'll be talking about beforehand, to keep you on topic.

Good lighting is essential. Make sure you are well-lit when you are filming. Handy tip: you can use tin foil to create a reflective light screen!

Look at the camera lens, not at yourself in the screen. Looking at the camera lens is the equivalent of making eye contact with your audience.

Pretend you are talking to your best friend. It makes it more natural to chat to a camera if you pretend it is someone you are comfortable talking to.

Video ideas:

Do a few takes, talk slowly, be yourself, work in some jokes and be ready to cut 20 minutes of footage into 3 minutes.

Pranks – if you do them right they can go viral instantly. Play jokes on your friends, family or poor unsuspecting members of the public and get ready for a giggle.

Feature videos – featuring your friends, your school, your wardrobe, family, pets, hobbies or even the contents of your bag – pick a topic and go with it. What's interesting to you will be interesting to others.

Challenge videos – FunForLouis wasn't always travelling the world, you know. He started out on YouTube eating gross food. The harder or funnier the challeng the more hits you may get.

TANYA SAYS...

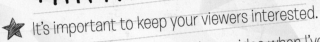

⭐ It's important to keep your viewers interested.

⭐ I make someone else watch my video when I've done a rough edit, then the bits that make me feel anxious that they're losing interest are the bits I cut out.

⭐ Put on a brave (and smiley) face. Try and act like you feel confident, even if you don't really.

ZOELLA SAYS...

♥ If you desperately want to make videos, and it's something you think you might enjoy, stuff what anyone else thinks!

♥ Be yourself. People follow me because I am just a normal person, and they can relate to me... I'm their virtual friend.

GRACE HELBIG SAYS...

● Commit. Have fun. Repeat.

● Make films you're passionate about.

● Passion and persistence can produce quality.

JOE SUGG SAYS...

⭐ Be original.

⭐ I've created a lot of video ideas that are brand new to YouTube. People tell me they like my channel because it's original.

ALFIE DEYES SAYS...

♥ Keep it real. I'm myself online, I'm not doing an act. I'm just talking to the people who watch my videos.

♥ Keep being active – nobody is going to be interested if you don't post any videos for years.

VSAUCE SAYS...

● Start making videos NOW. Even if they are terrible at first, you don't learn anything or get any better unless you're MAKING THEM.

● Make what you want to talk about. Believe it or not, a million other people (or more) probably want to join that conversation.

● Always be making stuff.

LILLY SINGH SAYS...

🐝 Don't try to be perfect. It's about relatability. I think what people like about my channel is that I am not perfect. I always point to my pimple, my bad hair day... people relate to that.

Life

Comedy

♫
Music

SUPERWOMAN

"Entertaining people makes me really happy."

SUPERSTAR ENTERTAINER!

| Timeline | **About** | Photos | Likes |

aka: Lilly Singh

born: 26 September 1988

tagline: Spent thousands of dollars on tuition, graduated and got a degree. I make YouTube videos now.

we ♥: her brilliant talent

she's like: the BFF every girl needs

most likely to: prove women can do anything and everything

least likely to: avoid an awkward subject

Almost all of Lilly's vlogs are based on people she knows. Many feature Manjeet and Paramjeet Singh, who are highly exaggerated portrayals of her father and mother.

FOLLOW HER ...

▶ IISuperwomanII, SuperwomanVlogs

🐦 @IISuperwomanII

📷 @iisuperwomanii

f /IISuperwomanII

Subscribers + 6 million

" ONE LOVE! "

BIO

The fearless and bold Lilly Singh tackles everything on her YouTube channel. From racism to the importance of sleep and her latest YouTube crush... no topic is too big, too small or too controversial for IISuperwomanII to vlog about. Funny, kind and understanding, Lilly totally gets what it's like to be embarrassed by our parents, have a tough time at school, and what emojis *really* mean, and she's guaranteed to put a smile on your face no matter how awkward the situation. Superwoman to the rescue!

Lilly loves visiting **India** and has a strong connection with her Punjabi heritage.

Her fans are known as **TEAM SUPER.**

5% **multiple characters**

5% **happy unicorn**

20% **positivity**

10% **butter popcorn addict**

10% **kind**

100% FUN!

30% **original**

20% **hilarious**

She's a woman of many talents... from creating videos to stand-up comedy, a clothing line, motivational speaking, rapping, event hosting and acting. It's no wonder she's called **Superwoman!**

▶ TOP WATCH...

Types of Teachers at School + 7.4 million views

▶

1996
Starts calling herself 'Superwoman' aged 8, after hearing it in a hip-hop song.

▶▶ **2010**
Launches her YouTube channel: IISuperwomanII.

▶▶ **2014**
Wins an Anokhi Media Award for 'Comedy Personality of the Year'.

▶▶ **2015**
Performs to live audiences on her worldwide tour, 'A Trip To Unicorn Island'.

Joey Graceffa

CENSORED

Timeline | **About** | **Photos** | **Likes**

aka: Joseph Michael Graceffa

born: 16 May 1991

tagline: My name is Joey! I vlog every single day!

we ♥: his funny collaboration videos

he's like: sweet and genuine

most likely to: become a movie star

least likely to: ever stop vlogging

▶ **Subscribers** + 4.9 million

" Well GOOD DAY, everyone."

" Oh my goodness gracianious! "

Joey dreams of becoming a MOVIE ACTOR.

FOLLOW HIM ...

▶ JoeyGraceffa, Joey Graceffa (games)

🐦 @JoeyGraceffa

📷 @joeygraceffa

f JoeyGraceffa

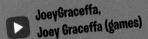
"LET'S BE NERDS TOGETHER!"

BROMANCE
Joey is good friends with vlogger **Shane Dawson**, even shipping himself with Shane as 'Shoey'.

BIO
Good looking, funny and always earnest, vlogger Joey Graceffa shares his hilarious observations on life with his millions of followers. He's also one of the busiest vloggers in the biz - despite uploading videos daily, he also manages to somehow squeeze in being a gaming vlogger, comedian, parody maker, model, singer-songwriter, actor, producer and book author too!

PET PALS
Joey loves his adorable husky dog named Wolf, who has one blue eye and one brown eye.

" May the odds be ever in your favour.
GOODBYE! "

2007
Uploads videos to the YouTube channel WinterSpringPro with his school friend Brittany Joyal.

2009
Creates his own YouTube channel, Joey Graceffa.

2013
Joey gains more and more popularity on YouTube and in American TV show, 'The Amazing Race'.

2014
Wins a Streamy Award for Best Actor in a Drama for his web series 'Storytellers'.

2015
Releases his book, 'In Real Life: My Journey to a Pixelated World'.

The SYNDICATE Project

CENSORED

UK GAMING GURU!

| Timeline | About | Photos | Likes |

aka: Tom Cassell

born: 23 June 1993

tagline: I love playing gaming and enjoy life to the maximum! Come take a peek at what I do!

we ♥: his random commentaries

he's like: a cool older brother

most likely to: sing whilst he's commentating

least likely to: miss a gaming convention

BIO

Tom Cassell had no idea that his passion for gaming would soon become his full-time job when he started posting his entertaining video game commentaries online back in 2010. Thankfully for us, he ignored his dad's advice to stop 'wasting time' playing the likes of Call of Duty, Halo and Minecraft, and quickly racked up a huge following. As well as talking to camera about games and life, Tom also lets us in on his travels around the world, visits to gaming conventions and his love of extreme sports. It's no wonder he's now the most subscribed to gaming commentator in the UK!

▶ **Subscribers** + 9 million

Tom has his own clothing line called Syndicate Original.

He dyed h... hair blue f... charity!

" Syndicate's Shenanigans!"

10% generous

10% world traveller

30%... natural tale...

10% adrenaline junkie

100% GAMER!

40% gaming geek

FOLLOW HIM ...

▶ The Syndicate Project, SyndicateCentral

🐦 @ProSyndicate

📷 @mrsyndicate

f /TheSyndicateProject

HOW TO GET AHEAD

Work hard, save hard! Tom bought his first filming equipment with money he earned from his job at McDonalds, where he had a part-time job before he was famous.

PET PALS

The gaming guru lives with a lizard named Steeve.

TOP WATCH...

Minecraft: Hunger Games

+ 4 million views

Comedy

Music

Miranda Sings

SINGING SENSATION!

Timeline | **About** | **Photos** | **Likes**

aka: Colleen Ballinger

born: 21 November 1986

tagline: Everyone tells me I have the best voice of all their friends.

we ❤ **:** her weird quirks

she's like: the worst singer ever

most likely to: overestimate her abilities

least likely to: listen to critics

FOLLOW HER ...

▶ Miranda Sings

🐦 @MirandaSings

📷 @MirandaSingsOfficial

f /MirandaSingsOfficial

▶ **Subscribers** + 4.2 million

"Hey guys, it's me, Miranda."

Miranda says her inspirations are Britney Spears, Avril Lavigne, the Spice Girls and, of course, Josh Groban.

"HATERS BACK OFF!"

Miranda
LOVES
her Mirfandas!

20% bad voice

10% wonky lipstick

20% unusually active eyebrows

10% determined

100% FUNNY!

40% hilarious

BIO

Miranda Sings was created by actress, singer and comedian Colleen Ballinger as a kind of anti-hero for YouTube. Poking fun at some of the people she had seen on YouTube trying to get famous, Colleen came up with her own creation and uploaded videos of the comically talentless, self-absorbed and quirky Miranda Sings. She dances badly, sings terribly, gives inept 'tutorials', rants about her critics, the haters, and more often than not gets the wrong end of the stick ... but we absolutely love her anyway!

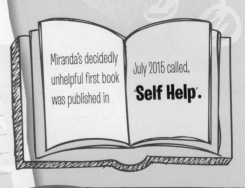
Miranda's decidedly unhelpful first book was published in July 2015 called, **'Self Help'**.

She likes to **lick** the air when she smells something she **likes**.

Life

Travel

JACKSGAP

THE TWINS!

Timeline   About   Photos   Likes

aka: Jackson Frayn Harries and Finnegan Frayn Harries

born: 13 May 1993

tagline: A storytelling project inspired by travel.

we ♥ : their inspirational videos

they're like: double the fun

most likely to: turn their bedroom into a ball pit

least likely to: have a family feud

▶ **Subscribers** + 4.1 million

"JACKSGAP, JACKSGAP, 5 MINUTES OF YOUR LIFE THAT YOU WON'T GET BACK."

DID YOU KNOW?

At first, Finn was reluctant to join his brother on YouTube. We're certainly glad he changed his mind!

" Finn, Finn, the better twin.
Jack, Jack, the better chap."

2011
Jack posts his first vlog in July – the first week of his gap year.

2012
In April, the brothers become YouTube partners as they hit 10,000 subscribers.

2013
They reach 1 million subscribers in February.

2013
Film a charity rickshaw race across India for Cancer Research, raising over $180,000.

BIO

Jack discovered YouTube while avoiding revision for his A-levels and later came up with the idea for his own channel in his gap year (hence the name JacksGap). What began as a way of documenting his gap year for friends and family to watch soon turned into a full-time job as more and more people tuned in. When Jack introduced his twin for the first time in one of his vlogs, his subscriber numbers nearly doubled. Realising that two was better than one, Finn began to make more appearances in his brother's vlogs and is now a co-owner of the channel. Today, the talented film-making twins continue to vlog and blog together about the world around them.

Finn is older than Jack by two minutes.

25% travel stories

20% inspiring

100% **DOUBLE TROUBLE!**

15% generous

30% twin-factor

10% creative

Entertainment is in their genes – Jack and Finn's dad is a TV producer and their mum is a director-turned-scriptwriter.

TOP WATCH...

The one where Jack introduced viewers to Finn for the first time!

My Brother Finn + 7.8 million views

"CHEEKY!"

Not only are the brothers super vlogger extraordinnaires, they're super charitable too, raising funds and awareness for causes they admire.

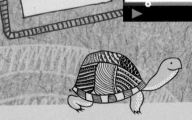

PET PALS
Jack and Finn have two tortoises, called Herbert and Doris.

FOLLOW THEM ...

 JacksGap

 @JacksGap

 @jacksgap

 /Jacksgap

2013
Jack and Finn start their company, Digital Natives Studio.

2014
JacksGap win two Screenchart! Channel Awards including 'Best Directing' and 'Best Mini-Series or Short Film' for 'The Rickshaw Run' videos.

2015
JacksGap post a video called 'Let's Talk About Mental Health' that was later referenced in an article on The Huffington Post.

WHAT NEXT?

39

GET CONNECTED

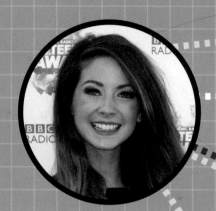

ZOELLA

POINTLESSBLOG

THATCHERJOE

AMAZINGPHIL

NIOMI SMART

SPRINKLEOFGLITTER

DANISNOTONFIRE

The more you discover about your favourite vloggers, the more you'll realise they're just one big happy family! Meet the close-knit British YouTube crew and get connected!

TANYA BURR

CASPAR LEE

TOM FLETCHER

JIM CHAPMAN

MARCUS BUTLER

PIXIWOO

ITSWAYPASTMYBEDTIME

············· COUPLE

············· BFFS!

············· ROOMMATES

············· RELATED

41

Life

Comedy

Caspar Lee

THE PRANKSTER!

Timeline | **About** | **Photos** | **Likes**

Subscribers +4.5 million

aka: Caspar Richard Lee

born: 24 April 1994

tagline: Guaranteed to make you laugh.

we ♥: his funny ways

he's like: quirky and loveable

most likely to: share his life with the world

least likely to: keep quiet about anything

"HI, my name is Caspar Lee."

Caspar admits to spending an awful lot of his time sleeping. ZZZZZZ!

"At the moment I'm the HAPPIEST I've ever lived in my life. I'm literally living the dream."

1994
Caspar is born in London, but moves to South Africa at a young age.

2010
Begins uploading videos on to YouTube because he was bored.

2011
Becomes known as Dicasp and creates his channel of the same name in November.

2012
Decides to move to London to focus on making a living from YouTube.

42

BIO

Meet Caspar Lee, everybody's favourite South African scamp! Caspar used to spend hours watching YouTubers online before deciding to make his first video (which he says was terrible) at the age of 16. Things have changed a bit since then – with over 4 million subscribers Caspar is now part of the YouTube elite and fans can't get enough of his unique brand of comedy and hilarious insights into his life. Turns out vlogging isn't his only talent – he can also add movie roles, stand-up comedy shows, and radio and TV appearances to his ever growing CV.

ROOMIES

Caspar shares a London flat with his pal and fellow YouTuber, **Joe Sugg**. They regularly feature in each other's videos where there's never a dull moment – expect plenty of pranks, shouting and all round silliness! Watch the one where Caspar tells Joe he's moving out, then laugh as Joe gets his own back in style (hint: it involves LOTS of Post-it notes!).

TOP WATCH...

Breaking up with my Roommate
+ 4.8 million views

30%
cheeky

15%
wild hair

% **cute accent**

100%
COMEDY KING!

10%
pranking genius

40%
funny

HOW TO GET AHEAD

Thinking of starting your own YouTube channel? Read on for Caspar's top tips...

✳ Make friends with other YouTubers on the same level and support each other.

✳ Just have fun. You've got to enjoy what you're doing.

✳ If it goes nowhere, then refresh yourself and keep persevering.

> " I get to do what I love every day. What more could I ask for?"

FOLLOW HIM ...

▶ Caspar, morecaspar

🐦 @Caspar_Lee

📷 @caspar_lee

f /casplee

> Caspar's sister, Theodora Lee, is also a YouTuber and regularly appears in his vlogs.

2014
Caspar stars as Garlic in the movie 'Spud 3: Learning to Fly', alongside fellow YouTuber Troye Sivan.

2014
Moves in with friend and vlogger, Joe Sugg.

2015
Voices Seagull #2 in the 'The SpongeBob Movie: Sponge Out of Water'.

2015
Visits Uganda to raise money for Comic Relief in March.

THE FINE BROS

MOST EXPERIENCED VLOGGERS!

Timeline | **About** | **Photos** | **Likes**

aka: Benny and Rafi Fine

born: 19 March 1982 (Benny) and 9 June 1984 (Rafi)

tagline: Comedy and series from Fine Brothers Entertainment.

we ♥ : that they're showing the youngsters how it's done!

they're like: the cool uncles of the Internet

most likely to: spoil the end of a movie

least likely to: run out of ideas for React videos

BIO

Brothers Benny and Rafi Fine had been making videos together for years before hitting Internet gold with their REACT YouTube series. They find all manner of weird and wonderful things on the web and film people's reactions to it, from viral videos to popular songs, YouTube stars and national news. The simple but hilarious idea took off, and what started off as Kids React has since expanded to Teens, Elders, YouTubers and Celebrities React, too. The hard working bros now have several awards under their belts, a TV series and feature films in the works.

▶ **Subscribers** +12.5 million

As kids, the brothers would entertain their friends with short sketches shot with action figures.

" *Quality Internet video!* "

TheFineBros have a YouTube empire, with over **25** people working for them!

▶ **TOP WATCH...**

AHHHHH!!!

Teens React to PewDiePie!
+ 28 million views

FOLLOW THEM...

▶ TheFineBros, REACT, TheFineBros2, MyMusic

🐦 @thefinebros

📷 @finebros

f /TheFineBros

2004 Upload their first video to the Internet.

2007 Create TheFineBros channel on YouTube.

2009 Launch a second channel on YouTube, called TheFineBros2.

2012 Win the Daytime Emmy award for 'Best Viral Video Series' for 'Kids React'.

2013 Win a Streamy Award for 'Best Non-Fiction or Reality Series' for 'Kids React'.

2014 Launch their first TV show 'React To That' on Nickelodeon.

2015 Taking their talent to the big screen, the brothers are writing, directing and producing a feature-length teen comedy.

BEST DOUBLE ACT!

Good Mythical MORNING

THE INTERNETAINERS!

Timeline | **About** | **Photos** | **Likes**

aka: Rhett James Mclaughlin and Charles Lincoln Neal III

born: 11 October 1977 (Rhett) and 1 June 1978 (Link)

tagline: We are Rhett and Link, and this is our daily morning talk show, Good Mythical Morning.

we ♥: their insane behaviour

they're like: constantly making fun of each other

most likely to: say whatever pops into their heads

least likely to: make any sense!

▶ **Subscribers** +7 million

The pals are known to perform live musical comedy and have completed over 100 songs and 5 albums!

Both Rhett and Link have degrees in Engineering, and were even roommates at University!

BIO

Famous for their amazingly funny songs, sketches and viral ads, Rhett and Link have been best friends since their first year at school. They entertain their millions of followers with a unique mixture of parodies, slapstick humour and actual useful information in their hugely popular daily YouTube show, Good Mythical Morning. If you've ever wanted to learn 5 Strange Facts About Bellybuttons, or see the 26 Craziest Selfies on the Internet (let's face it, who hasn't?), Rhett & Link are your guys.

" Laughter is like farting, out of your mouth."

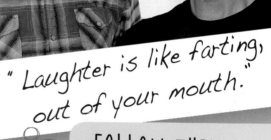

Their large following of fans are known as MYTHICAL BEASTS.

FOLLOW THEM ...

▶ Good Mythical Morning, Rhett & Link, Good Mythical MORE

🐦 @rhettandlink

📷 @rhettandlink

f /RhettAndLink

Good Mythical Morning is actually Rhett & Link's second YouTube channel, which became more popular than their original channel.

2006
Launch the Rhett & Link channel on YouTube.

2008
Launch their Good Mythical Morning YouTube channel.

2009
Create the 'Fast Food Folk Song' as a web ad for Taco Bell, and win an award for it.

2012
Named #2 on Business Insider's 'Top 25 Most Creative People in Advertising' list.

2013
Launch an audio podcast called 'Ear Biscuits', which features discussions with all kinds of media makers.

2014
Win 2 Screenchart! Channel Awards - 'Best Male Personality (Duo)' and 'Best Musical Performances'.

WHAT KIND OF VLOGGER WOULD YOU BE?

Take this test to see what type of vlogging you'd be best at!

1. Your friends would describe you as...
- a. happy
- b. ambitious
- c. original
- d. funny

2. What is the one thing you can't be without?
- a. your bag
- b. music
- c. gaming console
- d. your friends

3. If you could meet one YouTuber who would it be?
- a. Tanya Burr
- b. Tyler Oakley
- c. Stampylonghead
- d. Marcus Butler

4. What do you love to do in your spare time?
- a. shop till you drop
- b. daydream about the future
- c. play computer games
- d. hang out with your mates

5. Which vlogger would you most like to collab with?
- a. SprinkleofGlitter
- b. ItsWayPastMyBedTime
- c. Smosh
- d. ThatcherJoe

6. How would you describe your style?
- a. stylish
- b. a trendsetter
- c. don't care
- d. casual

7. Your favourite type of movie is...

- [ ] a. a romantic comedy
- [ ] b. a Disney classic
- [ ] c. a scary horror film
- [ ] d. an action adventure

8. Your life's ambition is to...

- [ ] a. work in fashion
- [ ] b. star in a movie
- [ ] c. create video games
- [ ] d. make everyone laugh

Mostly As:

You'd be a brilliant beauty and fashion vlogger! Your vlogs should be all about you – your life, your friends, your hauls and your amazing style.

Mostly Bs:

You're a born entertainer! Whether it's singing, dancing or acting you love best, reach for the stars and showcase your talents online.

Mostly Cs:

You're a gaming guru! Turn your addiction for gaming into cool vlog content and show the world how to play the games you love, just like top gamer PewDiePie!

Mostly Ds:

Don't waste that sense of humour – you're clearly a comedy star! Entertain your viewers with pranks, jokes and your zany take on life!

Life

Comedy

CONNOR FRANTA

THE ENTREPRENEUR!

About

Timeline | **About** | **Photos** | **Likes**

aka: Connor Joel Franta

born: 12 September 1992

tagline: I talk to my camera.

we ♥: his honesty

he's like: funny but serious all at the same time

most likely to: be courageous

least likely to: recommend a bad song

▶ **Subscribers** **+ 4.5 million**

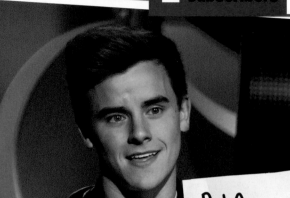

He was a lifeguard for six years and has saved two lives.

▶ TOP WATCH...

So I Googled Myself... + 4 million views

"You are who you are and you should love that person."

"FRANTASTIC!"

BIO

After achieving success on the teen dream collab channel 'Our2ndLife', Connor broke away to create his own YouTube channel, creating down-to-earth vlogs chatting to camera about anything and everything that interests him in life, from relationships to music. Building on his online success, this hard-working, entrepreneurial vlogger is busy creating his own offline empire too, with his own coffee brand, clothing line, book, music and charity projects in the works.

PET PALS

Connor's obsessed with cats and he owns two, one called Pre and one called Sam. **MEOW**

Connor has impeccable taste in music. He uses his fame to share and promote talented undiscovered artists, and his dream for the future is to produce and manage up-and-coming musical talent.

FOLLOW HIM ...

 ConnorFranta

 @ConnorFranta

 @connorfranta

 /ConnorFrantaFans

2010
Uploads his first video to YouTube in August.

2012
Joins collab channel Our2ndLife and becomes widely known.

2014
Leaves Our2ndLife.

2014
Releases his first music album 'Crown' featuring all his favourite new artists.

2014
Launches The Thirst Project to build wells for people in Swaziland.

2015
Releases his own brand of coffee called Common Culture Coffee.

2015
His first book, 'A Work in Progress', hits the shops in April.

Life

Travel

FUN for LOUIS

MOST ADVENTUROUS!

| Timeline | **About** | Photos | Likes |

aka: Louis John Cole

born: 28 April 1983

tagline: I enjoy travelling the world with friends, having fun and inspiring others!

we ♥ : how he inspires us

he's like: a big kid at heart

most likely to: visit every country in the entire world

least likely to: stay in one place for too long

He hates **cold** weather.

Louis loves making friends from different cultures and learning from them. He's also friends with all the YouTube gang!

Louis always vlogs daily no matter what the day or what he's feeling. **That's commitment!**

Subscribers + 1.4 million

ALFIE

LOUISE

" Peace out, enjoy life, live the adventure. "

BIO

It's hard not to be jealous of Louis Cole, who has been able to travel the world for a living by turning his thirst for adventure into a huge online following. Creating vlogs from the far-flung corners of the globe, Louis loves to inspire his followers to get outside, explore and enjoy life. This modern day explorer has also turned his love of travel into a passion for fashion with his own clothing line called 'Find the Nomad'.

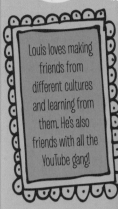

40% travelling nomad

5% slick production

100% NOMAD!

20% coffee addict

10% kind

10% double-decker bus owner

15% hot tub fan

He originally found fame eating gross things on his YouTube channel, FoodForLouis.

EUGHHH!

TOP WATCH...

Epic World Adventure + 2 million views

The one that will make you want to see the world!

" Creating the best stories and flooding the world with memories. "

FOLLOW HIM ...

▶ FunForLouis

🐦 @funforlouis

📷 @funforlouis

f /FunForLouis

MARCUS BUTLER TV

THE CHEEKY ONE!

Timeline | **About** | **Photos** | **Likes**

aka: Marcus Lloyd Butler

born: 18 December 1991

tagline: Part time rapper. Full time vlogger and food lover.

we ♥ : his silly sense of humour

he's like: sweet and trustworthy

most likely to: say 'Helloooooo'

least likely to: take life seriously

Subscribers + 3.8 million

"HELLOOOO!"

"I'M JUST A NORMAL BOY."

Marcus has his own clothing line which he sells on his website.

" If you have a dream or if you have a passion ... don't stop, go for it!"

2010
Creates his YouTube channel in January.

2012
Gets his chest waxed in January to celebrate hitting 20,000 subscribers.

2012
Hits 100,000 subscribers by September, and stands on top of a plane to celebrate the milestone.

2013
Creates the YouTube boyband with Joe Sugg, Jim Chapman and Alfie Deyes (Caspar Lee joined later).

BIO

Drawn to the Internet from an early age, Marcus started out his YouTube career by posting music mixes and edited sports footage online. His comments sections were soon filled with viewers requesting him to upload videos of himself, so he decided to give it a go and MarcusButlerTV was born! His weekly vlogs are a fun and entertaining mixture of his views on life, hilarious pranks, sketches, and advice, earning him over 3 million subscribers, and a whole lot of love.

120 Chicken Nuggets in 20 Minutes
+ 2.5 million views

Marcus is totally terrified of bees and wasps.

BEST BUDS

Malfie is the collab' name for Marcus and his best mate Alfie Deyes. They love nothing better than collaborating on challenge videos, funny sketches and attempts to break world records. **#BROMANCE**

15% funny

5% loves food

5% music fan

100% CHEEKY!

40% likes to chat

10% challenges

10% great hair

15% sports fan

Marcus holds the world record for the 'most bangles put on in 30 seconds by a team of two', along with YouTubers Alfie Deyes and Laurbubble.

"You guys are **incredible.** Thank you so, so much for sticking with **me** and **watching** these videos!"

CUTE COUPLE ALERT!

Collectively known as **Narcus**, Marcus and his gorg' girlfriend **Niomi Smart** (who has her own channel) have been dating since they were at school, although their romance wasn't revealed to fans until 2012. They now collaborate on lots of videos and live together in London.

FOLLOW HIM ...

 Marcus Butler, MoreMarcus

 @MarcusButlerTv

 @marcusbutler

 /MarcusButlerTV

2013
Becomes a member of the Guinness World Records YouTube channel alongside Alfie Deyes.

2014
Sings in the YouTube boyband video 'It's All About You(tube)' for Comic Relief.

2015
Releases his first book 'Hello Life!' sharing his trademark big-brotherly advice in written form.

HERE WE GOOOO!

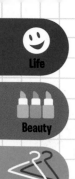

Life

Beauty

Fashion

Niomi Smart

LIFESTYLE **PRINCESS!**

Timeline | **About** | **Photos** | **Likes**

aka: Niomi Smart

born: 26 May 1992

tagline: I film and write about my passions. Fashion. Food. Health. Beauty.

we ❤ : her amazing hair

she's like: SUPER girly

most likely to: eat healthily

least likely to: skip the gym

▶ **Subscribers** + 1.3 million

Niomi is good friends with fellow beauty vlogger **Tanya Burr.**

BIO

Niomi was introduced to the wonderful world of vlogging by her boyf, Marcus Butler. After featuring in lots of his videos and getting great comments from fans, she decided to go it alone and upload some of her own. Vlogging about all things fashion, beauty and healthy lifestyle related, with a sprinkling of funny stuff mixed in, Niomi has quickly built up a large following of loyal fans.

" I just love it."

▶ TOP WATCH...

My Morning Routine
+ 2.4 million hits

This girl is rapidly rising up the YouTube ranks. After posting just two vids on her channel, she'd already gained **100,000** subscribers and become a full-on Internet fashionista!

20% super nice

10% make-up master

10% style inspo

100% FUNNY!

20% long swishy hair

40% healthy living

FOLLOW HER ...

▶ **Niomi Smart**

@niomismart

@niomismart

/NiomiSmart

52

Troye Sivan

CENSORED

SUPER TALENTED!

Life

Music

"I feel like being NICE to others is the coolest thing anyone can be."

Timeline	**About**	Photos	Likes

aka: Troye Sivan Mellet

born: 5 June 1995

tagline: That guy from the songs/movies/videos/Australia.

we ♥: his awesome music

he's like: a YouTube sensation about to hit IRL stardom

most likely to: write a song about how he feels

least likely to: forget to ring his mum

▶ **Subscribers** **+ 3.4 million**

"You're all beautiful. And you shouldn't let anyone tell you otherwise."

"I'M ANGRY BECAUSE IT'S NOT SOCIALLY ACCEPTABLE TO WEAR MY ONESIE IN PUBLIC."

Troye's younger brother, Tyde Levi, is also on YouTube.

He began his YouTube channel when he was just 12 years old.

BIO

This South African-born, Australian bred vlogger, singer, songwriter and actor has rocketed to success on YouTube thanks to his insanely good singing voice, great acting skills, good looks and hyperactive entertaining chatter. His vlogs, films and music have quite deservedly gained him millions of fans and followers all over the world, with his first single 'Happy Little Pill' attracting over 7 million YouTube views alone. If you're not already on the Troye bandwagon, jump on it now - this boy is going places.

FOLLOW HIM ...

▶ **Troye Sivan**

🐦 **@troyesivan**

📷 **@troyesivan**

f **/troyesivan**

Troye **loves** chocolate spread but hates tomatoes.

▶ **TOP WATCH...**

Troyler

Troye's friendship with Tyler Oakley has spawned its own fandom, shipping the pair as Troyler and winning them a Teen Choice Award for their video, **'The Boyfriend Tag'**.

2007
Joins YouTube.

2009
Cast as a young Wolverine in 'X-Men Origins: Wolverine' after his videos caught the eye of a Hollywood agent.

2009
Wins the lead role in the movie franchise 'Spud'.

2013
Signs a music deal with EMI Australia, but keeps it a secret for a whole year.

2014
Releases his EP entitled 'TRXYE', going to the top of the iTunes chart in 55 different countries.

2014
Wins a Teen Choice Award for 'Choice Web Collaboration', and a NewNowNext award for 'Best New Social Media Influencer'.

2015
Wins the Kid's Choice Award for 'Favourite Aussie/Kiwi Internet Sensation'.

Life

Fashion

Beauty

Bethany Mota

QUEEN OF THE HAUL!

Timeline | **About** | **Photos** | **Likes**

aka: Bethany Noel Mota

born: 7 November 1995

tagline: My viewers are my besties.

we 🖤 : her upbeat sweet nature

she's like: happy all the time

most likely to: show you how to make something

least likely to: skip a shopping trip

▶ **Subscribers** +8.8 million

"BeYOU(tiful)!"

Bethany loves the movies **Frozen** and **Despicable Me.**

" Be who you are and say what you feel because those who mind don't matter and those who matter don't mind."

2009
Starts her YouTube channel in order to escape the stress of bullying.

2013
Launches a clothing and accessories line at Aéropostale, a clothing shop for teens.

2014
Selected to appear in YouTube's first advertising campaign.

2014
Makes it to the finals of 'Dancing with the Stars' (the US version of 'Strictly Come Dancing').

2014
Releases a single called 'Need you Right Now' in October.

54

BIO

Sweet and caring Bethany Mota rose to fame off the back of her haul, beauty and fashion vlogs after launching her YouTube channel when she was just 13. Since then she has released original music, interviewed President Obama and even oversees her own clothing line! She is adored by millions and loves to interact with her fans on her tours.

TOP WATCH...

The one to give you some room-spiration!

Easy ways to spice up your room! + DIY Decorations + 10 million views

Bethany was a guest judge on season 13 of **Project Runway**.

20% make-up and hair tutorials

25% outfit inspiration

5% adorable

100% BEAUTIFUL!

20% DIY ideas

30% hauls

Beth calls her fans **Mota-vators**.

FOLLOW HER ...

▶ Macbarbie07, BethanysLife

🐦 @BethanyMota

📷 @bethanynoelm

f /Bethany-Mota

Her favourite colour is **pink**.

DID YOU KNOW?
Bethany's older sister Brittany is also a popular YouTuber.

2014
Wins a Teen Choice Award for 'Choice Web Star: Female'.

2014
Wins a Streamy Award for 'Best Fashion Program'.

2014
Is named one of the '25 Most Influential Teens of 2014' by Time magazine.

2015
Interviews President Barack Obama in January.

2015
Confirms in May that she is working on new music, and possibly a new album!

55

Life

Music

ItsWayPast MyBedTime

Talent runs in the Fletcher family - Carrie's big bro is **McFly's** (and supergroup McBusted's) Tom Fletcher!

THE **GIRL** WE WANT TO BE!

| Timeline | About | Photos | Likes |

aka: Carrie Hope Fletcher

born: 22 October 1992

tagline: Usually happy. Always eating cake.

we ♥ : her warm and caring attitude

she's like: the big sis you need in your life

most likely to: give you goosebumps with her voice

least likely to: dish out bad advice

▶ **Subscribers** + 600K

"I WEAR ODD SOCKS. ALL THE TIME. EVERY DAY."

She started acting when she was just 6 years old.

BIO

The Brit-born vlogging sensation is something of an all-rounder. Singer, songwriter, actress, musician, blogger, author – you name it, Carrie Hope Fletcher can do it. When Carrie's not playing Éponine in 'Les Misérables' in London, she's recording vlogs and acting as an 'honorary big sister' to thousands of young people who turn to her for her heartfelt advice and friendship, tackling tough topics such as bullying, body image, relationships and growing up.

SHHHH!
Carrie gets really bad stage fright. Who'd have thought it!

"Don't ditch your childhood dreams just because you dreamt them up as a child."

FOLLOW HER ...

▶ ItsWayPastMyBedTime, TwentyThirtyTwo.

🐦 @CarrieHFletcher

📷 @carriehopefletcher

f /ItsWayPastMyBedTime

▶ TOP WATCH...

Boys in Books are Better
+ 725,000 views

HARRY POTTER
HUNGER GAMES
TWILIGHT
PRIDE & PREJUDICE

5% trampoline fanatic

5% Disney addict

20% book lover

20% kind and caring

100% FABULOUS!

50% super talented

2011
Posts her first video on YouTube in March.

2014
Plays Beth in the final arena tour of Jeff Wayne's 'The War of the Worlds'.

2014
In March fellow YouTuber Pete Bucknall (petesjams) tweets the news that he and Carrie are a couple.

2014
Wins WhatsOnStage Award for 'Best Takeover in a Role' in recognition of her performance in 'Les Miserables'.

2015
Releases her first book, 'All I Know Now: Wonderings and Reflections on Growing up Gracefully'.

charlieissocoollike

MR NICE GUY!

" I wish I had more quotes to put here."

Timeline | **About** | **Photos** | **Likes**

aka: Charles Joseph McDonnell

born: 1 October 1990

tagline: So there was this one time when I made a video about tea and now YouTube is my job or something.

we ♥ : his everyday ordinariness

he's like: totally engaging, silly and fun

most likely to: tell you something you don't know

least likely to: stick to one topic

Charlie has many famous fans, including **Matt Smith, John Green** and **Stephen Fry!**

▶ **Subscribers** **+ 2.4 million**

BIO

He may be embarrassed that he's never had a 'proper' job (he started making videos while he was meant to be revising and didn't ever stop!), but fans around the world are very happy Charlie devotes his time to vlogging and sharing his views on literally everything with them instead. This British vlogger is multi-talented – as well as vlogging everything from sketches and songs to science and short films, and being an all-round 'really nice guy', he's also branched out to working with charities, hosting radio shows and even making an album!

DID YOU KNOW?

Charlie was the first vlogger in the UK to reach **1 million subscribers** on YouTube!

" Laughing is easily my second favourite thing. After eating."

His current girlfriend is Emily Diana Ruth, another fellow YouTuber and filmmaker.

"AH, THE TELEVISION. JUST LIKE THE INTERNET, BUT NOT AS GOOD."

PET PALS

Charlie loves to vlog about his cat Gideon who he reckons lives up to his name, which means 'destroyer'!

FOLLOW HIM ...

 charlieissocoollike, charlieissoboredlike

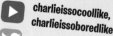 @coollike

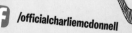 @coollike

 /officialcharliemcdonnell

2007
Launches his YouTube channel in April.

2008
Showcases his music with a song called 'Blink'.

2010
Releases his first album, 'This is Me'.

2011
Becomes the first UK channel to reach 1 million subscribers.

2013-4
Makes four short films, funded by YouTube.

2015
Plays the main voice role in the video game 'Volume'.

QUALI TEA

VLOGGING BY NUMBERS

10
= YouTube celebrated its 10th anniversary in 2015.

2
= The number of guinea pigs owned by Zoella.

61 million
= The number of views (so far) on Jenna Marbles' video – 'How To Trick People into Thinking You're Good Looking'.

12
= The age Troye Sivan was when he first started vlogging. Awwww!

3
= Zoella's shoe size. Teeny!

7
= The number of days a week that Stampylonghead uploads a new gaming video.

4
= The number of vloggers in the Chapman family.

1982
= The year Benny Fine (from TheFineBros) was born in, making him one of the oldest YouTubers who has more than 10 million subscribers.

1
= PewDiePie is the No 1 most-subscribed to vlogger in the world.

1,565
= The record for the highest number of vlogs posted consecutively, by Charles and Alli Trippy from the 'Internet Killed Television' YouTube channel.

191
= danisnotonfire's height in centimetres.

Life

Comedy

Grace Helbig

"Be the weirdest little weird in all Weird Town."

Timeline | **About** | **Photos** | **Likes**

aka: Grace Anne Helbig

born: 27 September 1985

tagline: What a charming idiot.

we ♥ : her unique sense of humour

she's like: an awkward older sister

most likely to: dance like no one's watching even though *everyone* is watching

least likely to: pretend to be something she's not

▶ **Subscribers** + 2.5 million

Grace says her favourite YouTuber is Miranda Sings.

Her **BFF** is super successful 'Tuber **Hannah Hart.**

Grace released her first book, 'Grace's Guide: The Art of Pretending to be a Grown-up' in 2014.

Her second tongue-in-cheek book, 'Grace & Style' is due for release at the end of 2015!

" I'm OVERWHELMED by Internet feels."

BIO

With her perfect hair and kooky sense of humour, multi-talented Grace Helbig is one of our fave females on the web, and her 2 million loyal subscribers seem to agree. If you like your vloggers funny, relatable, pop-culture-friendly and a little on the weird side, then Grace is your girl. Rated as one of the sharpest and funniest voices on YouTube, she's even managed to make the jump from online star to offline fame and fortune with movie roles, a New York Times best-selling book and a TV show. Go Grace!

FOLLOW HER ...

▶ **Grace Helbig**

🐦 **@gracehelbig**

📷 **@gracehelbig**

f **/gracehelbig**

Grace started making YouTube videos in 2007 to cure boredom while she was housesitting.

WOOF!!

PET PALS

Grace's dog **Goose** is a cross between a bulldog and a Boston terrier and often appears in her videos.

Grace's brother Tim also has a YouTube channel called **TimWillDestroyYou.**

2006
Joins YouTube.

2013
Wins two Streamy Awards, one for 'Best First-Person Series' for Daily Grace and one for 'Audience Choice Personality of the Year'.

2014
Her first book is released in October.

2014
Stars in the film 'Camp Takota' alongside her pals Hannah Hart and Mamri Hart.

2015
Is named as one of the 'Most Influential People on the Internet' by Time Magazine.

2015
'The Grace Helbig Show' premieres on the E! network in April.

2015
Appears in 'SMOSH: The Movie', released in July.

STAMPY LONGHEAD

GAMING HERO!

Timeline | **About** | **Photos** | **Likes**

aka: Joseph Garrett

born: 13 December 1990

tagline: I like making YouTube videos and eating cake.

we 🖤 **:** that he posts new videos every day

he's like: your geeky game-obsessed older brother

most likely to: teach you how to play games

least likely to: swear or be rude online

His best friend is a squid. **iBallisticSquid** to be precise, played by fellow YouTuber, David Spencer. The pair team up on commentaries for double the fun.

▶ **Subscribers** + 5.9 million

15% shy

10% orange cat

20% funny

5% kid-friendly

100% GAMER!

50% gaming guru

BIO

Stampylonghead (also known as Stampy Cat, stampylongnose, or just plain Stampy), is an animated orange cat voiced by Joseph Garrett, who delivers witty commentary and hilarious one-liners in his Let's Play game tutorials. Stampy's popularity has been built on the back of the successful game Minecraft and the fact that he offers his millions of fans fresh fun on a daily basis. So great is his commentary that fans the world over often prefer watching him playing games to playing the games themselves!

SHHHH! Stampy is rumoured to be involved in an upcoming Minecraft film.

"I think I've got the best job in the world."

He has a degree in film and animation.

FOLLOW HIM ...

▶ stampylonghead, Wonder Quest

🐦 @stampylongnose

f /stampylongnose

2006
Starts first YouTube channel, Stampylongnose, posting music parodies and game reviews.

2011
Creates current channel, Stampylonghead to post a separate series of Minecraft videos.

2012
Slowly transitions to the newer, cleaner channel as popularity grows.

2013
Leaves his job as a barman to concentrate on YouTube full-time.

2014
Receives, on average, 3000 messages a day from viewers asking for gaming tips.

2014
Becomes one of the 10 most-watched channels on YouTube.

2015
Creates a new educational channel called Wonder Quest in collab' with Maker Studios.

VSAUCE

" I love SCIENCE and ART and HISTORY and LANGUAGE and MATH and PHILOSOPHY and making VIDEOS and THINGS."

Timeline | **About** | **Photos** | **Likes**

aka: Michael Stevens

born: 23 January 1986

tagline: The world is amazing.

we ♥ : his fantastic facts

he's like: the coolest nerd on the net

most likely to: blow your mind

least likely to: run out of inspiration

Michael studied both Neuropsychology and English Language and Literature. It's no wonder he's so good at stringing a scientific sentence together!

▶ **Subscribers** +8.9 million

Michael wanted a name for his channel that meant absolutely nothing, so it would always fit with whatever kind of videos he wanted to make.

An average Vsauce video takes about 7-9 days to make.

"Hey Vsauce, Michael here."

10% **super smart**

10% **teacher**

15% **curious**

100% **AMAZING!**

50% **inspiring**

15% **fascinating**

"STAY CURIOUS!"

▶ **TOP WATCH...**

What If Everyone JUMPED At Once? +16 million hits

Vsauce 1 is part of a collection of YouTube channels, with Vsauce 2 ('People are Awesome'), Vsauce 3 ('Fictional Worlds are Amazing'), and fan channel WeSauce.

BIO

Vsauce host, Michael Stevens, inspires and educates his millions of followers by investigating out-of-the-ordinary questions in totally bonkers ways. Whether it's exploring answers to the questions 'Why Do We Clap?', 'What If the Moon was a Disco Ball?', or 'Why Are Things Creepy?' – if you look at the world around you and want to know the whys, whats, wheres and the hows, Vsauce is the YouTube channel for you.

FUN FACT

Vsauce sounds like the Finnish word 'viisaus', meaning 'wisdom'.

His first YouTube channel was called **pooplicker888**.

FOLLOW HIM ...

▶ Vsauce1, Vsauce2, Vsauce3, WeSauce

🐦 @tweetsauce

📷 @electricpants

f /VsauceGaming

ONES TO WATCH

These lesser-known YouTubers may not have the same amount of subs' as the vlogging superstars just yet but they're certainly on their way!

ALLIE MARIE EVANS

LA filmmaker, Allie Marie Evans, is one of YouTube's top teen rising stars. She's loved for her creative fashion films, lookbooks and her girl-next-door charm. She's just an ordinary girl who, thanks to YouTube, can now share her extraordinary life with the world.

INTHEFROW

As a fashion doctorate graduate, Victoria Magrath (aka Inthefrow), knows her stuff when it comes to shooting her fashion and beauty videos. Her cool lilac hair and brilliant style are her trademarks.

CHERRY WALLIS

Birmingham-based Cherry Wallis is a rising star in the world of vlogging, where her alternative style and deadpan delivery make her stand out in a sea of uploads. Her first video, where she drank a mixture of Coke and milk, 'accidently went viral' with over 1 million views.

BOXES OF FOXES

Emma Blackery's latest channel, boxes of foxes, is ideal for anyone going through stuff with school, growing up and general tricky topics. Emma's on hand to have a friendly chat about it all and give out some of her smashing advice, as well as reviewing high street hauls. Everything you could ever need from a YouTuber, really.

OLI WHITE

Oli White is a British YouTuber who creates quirky comedy videos. His cool combo of challenges, collaborations and funny skits is gaining him fans fast.

BOOKS AND QUILLS

Sanne Vliegenthart puts her English degree and job in publishing to good use in her book reviewing YouTube channel. She's totally passionate about books and is bound to expand your reading horizons.